More people than I can count have supported me along my inflated journey. Friends and strangers have carried balloons for photographs, gate keepers have given me special permissions, and colleagues have helped me edit and refine the book. While any shortcomings remain my own, I am extremely blessed to have traveled with so many extraordinary people along the way.

A Fair Friend Publication
Pensacola, FL

ISBN 978-0-9979039-0-4
First Edition

www.inflatedstory.com

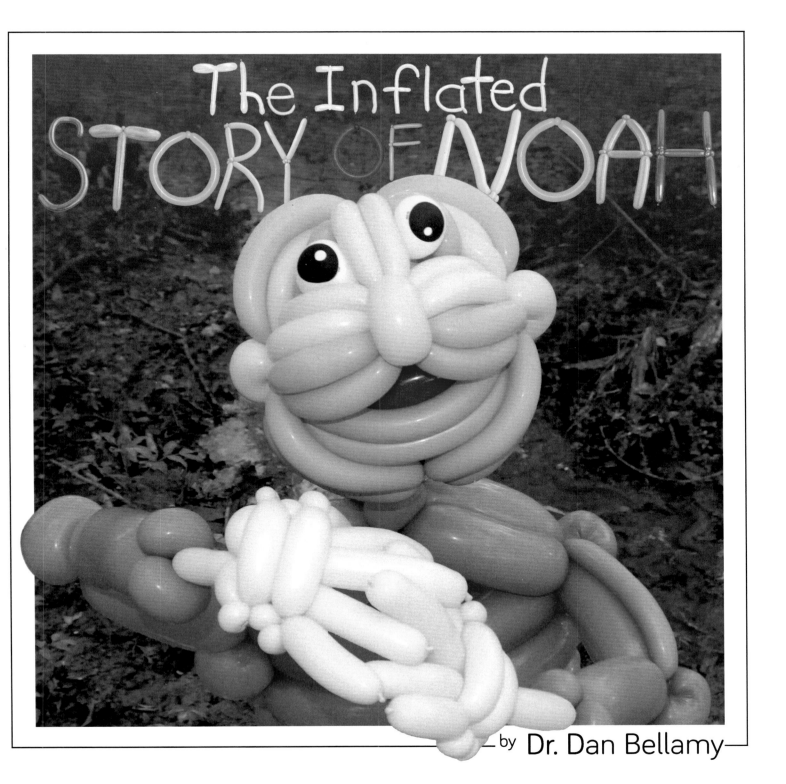

The Inflated STORY OF NOAH

by Dr. Dan Bellamy

In the beginning, God made the earth good, but before long people became hopelessly twisted by sin.

Mobile, AL

Thomasville, GA

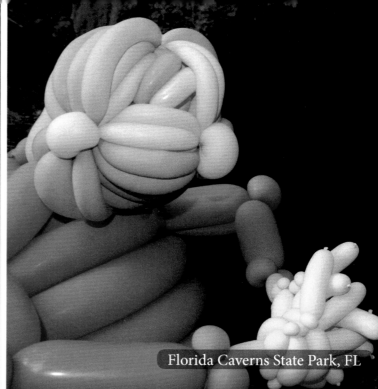
Florida Caverns State Park, FL

Even with all the evil in the world, there was one man, named Noah, who found favor in God's eyes. To save the world from sin, God told Noah to build an ark.

Thomasville, GA

Thomasville, GA

The ark would protect Noah's family and some of every animal from the coming flood.

Santa Maria Chiquimula, Guatemala

Santa Maria Chiquimula, Guatemala

Noah and his wife had three married sons named Shem, Ham, and Japheth to help with the labor ahead.

Santa Maria Chiquimula, Guatemala

Mount of Olives Jerusalem, Israel

Each and every family member had a task to do.

Some built, some gathered, and some planned.

The hard work stretched them, but it was worth it.

Mount of Olives Jerusalem, Israel

Thomasville, GA

Thomasville, GA

Florida Caverns State Park, FL

They needed to collect supplies for all the people and animals that were going to be on the ark.

Thomasville, GA

Marshall, TX

Marshall, TX

Marshall, TX

The family knew they would need plenty of food to get them through the months ahead.

Marshall, TX

Atlanta, TX

And, of course, it takes a LOT of wood to build a boat large enough to save the world.

Atlanta, TX

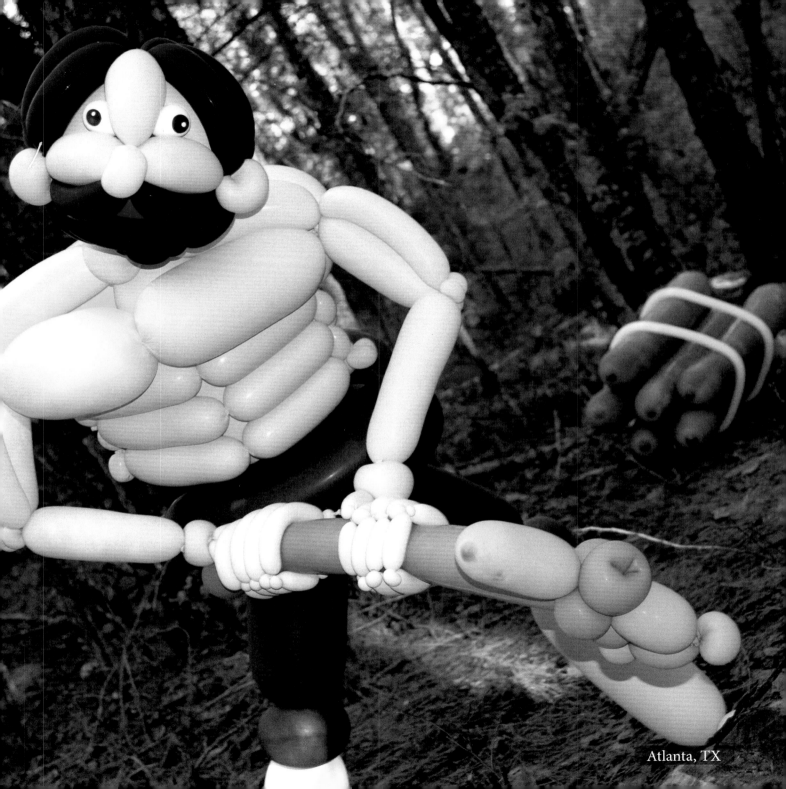

Atlanta, TX

Pensacola Beach, FL

God had Noah take along at least one male and one female of every animal in the world! In fact, God had Noah bring seven pairs of some animals.

There were giraffes, and lions, and bears, but they were just the beginning!

Pensacola Beach, FL

Pensacola Beach, FL

Pensacola Beach, FL

Pensacola Beach, FL

The **Moose** hoofed it into the ark.

Lake Ontario, Canada

Lake Ontario, Canada

The **Sheep**
knew it would be BAA-d
to miss the boat.

Chimney Rock, NC

The
Elephants
were sure to pack
their trunks.

Atlanta, TX

Atlanta, TX

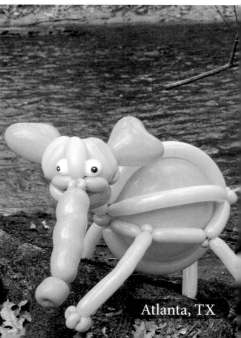

Atlanta, TX

Atlanta, TX

Kenai Fjords National park, AK

Seward, AK

The **Eagles**
decided to wing it.

Kenai Fjords National park, AK

Kenai Fjords National park, AK

The
Flamingos
flocked to the ark
in their best pink.

Floreana, Galapagos Islands

Floreana, Galapagos Islands

The Penguins
outdressed everyone
in their tuxedos.

Floreana, Galapagos Islands

Floreana, Galapagos Islands

The Iguanas

relaxed, knowing God was in control.

Punta Suarez, Galapagos Islands

Punta Suarez, Galapagos Islands

Santa Fe, Galapagos Islands

Santa Fe, Galapagos Islands

The # Sea Lions

were happy to have a place to land.

Punta Suarez, Galapagos Islands

Santa Fe, Galapagos Islands

Punta Suarez, Galapagos Islands

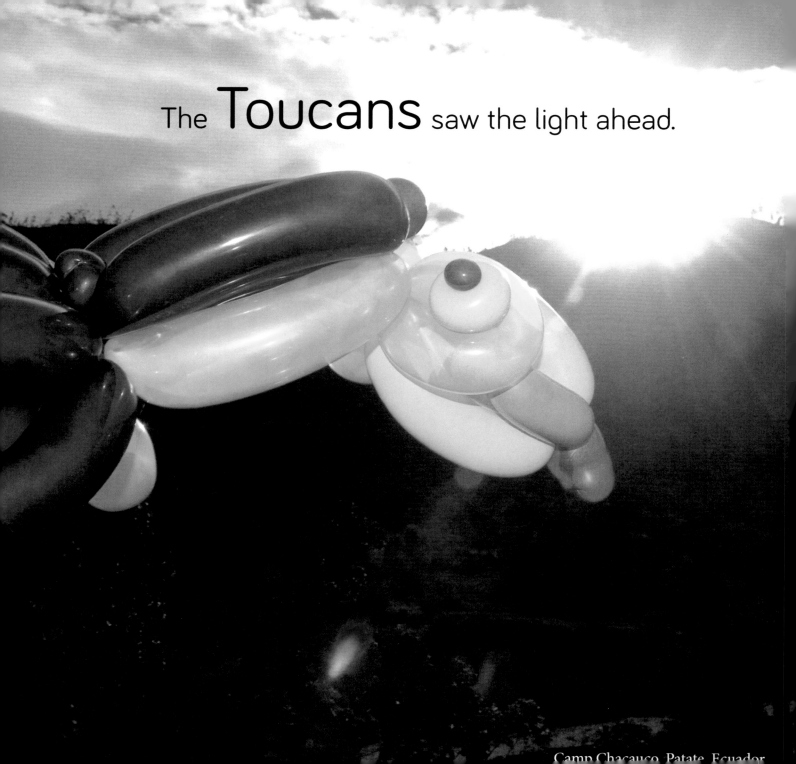

The **Toucans** saw the light ahead.

Camp Chacauco, Patate, Ecuador

Camp Chacauco, Patate, Ecuador

Even the
Tortoises
were sure
to be on time!

Santa Cruz, Galapagos Islands

Santa Cruz, Galapagos Islands

Santa Cruz, Galapagos Islands

Volcano Tungurahua, Ecuador

And the **Monkeys**
decided they better hang
around.

Sure enough,
at least two of
every animal
made it!

Ecuador

Finally, the Ark was completed, the animals and people were loaded, and God closed the door.

Then the clouds rolled in and the rains started.

Pensacola Beach, FL

And the **Alligators** said, "See you later!"

Everglades National Park, FL

Navarre Beach, FL

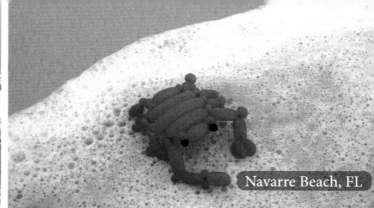

Navarre Beach, FL

At first, the Crabs were upset about missing the ark, but then they remembered they live underwater.

Navarre Beach, FL

Navarre Beach, FL

After the door was shut, it rained like never before. But Noah, his family, and the animals were safe on the ark.

Galveston, TX

Pensacola Beach, FL

When the downpour finally ended after forty days and forty nights, they waited for the earth to dry.

God had not forgotten about them!

Dead Sea, Israel

Navarre Beach, FL

After the rains, Noah sent out a raven that flew back and forth looking for land, but the earth had not dried yet.

Navarre Beach, FL

Navarre Beach, FL

Navarre Beach, FL

Later, he sent a dove, but it could not find a place to land. It returned with an empty beak.

Sea of Galilee, Israel

Sea of Galilee, Israel

After another week, Noah sent a second dove. That one returned with a freshly picked olive leaf!

Mount Precipice, Israel

Once they knew there was dry land, Noah and his family just needed to be patient.

Finally, the waters dried around them, and they were able to exit the ark. It had come to a rest on the mountains of Ararat.

Masada, Israel

Then God sent a sign to let Noah and his family know the world would never be destroyed this way again.

Megiddo, Israel

When we see the
rainbow, it is our
reminder of
God's promise...

We have
a new

been given
beginning!

Oak Mountain State Park, AL

Read the stories behind
the pictures at
www.inflatedstory.com

Made in the USA
Columbia, SC
13 February 2019